Declutter Your Mind

~The Yogic Way~

15 Ultimate Secrets of the Ancient Indian Seers to Eliminate Mental Clutter, get rid of Negative Thoughts, Relieve Anxiety and have a Peaceful Mind all the time.

by

Advait

Disclaimer and FTC Notice

Declutter Your Mind The Yogic Way: 15 Ultimate Secrets of the Ancient Indian Seers to Eliminate Mental Clutter, get rid of Negative Thoughts, Relieve Anxiety and have a Peaceful Mind all the time.

Content

Advait

Introduction

If you are familiar with my previous works, you know that I like to keep all my books fluff-free and concise. This one won't be any different.

I will not waste 20 pages telling you what mental clutter is; rather I would like you to tell you a simple analogy and how mental clutter affects us.

The Ancient Indian Vedic philosophy calls our mind as a monkey, but, it was in that era.

Today, with all the distractions, the 24 hr news, phone notifications, continuously ringing cell phones, it is the era of information overdose.

Our mind is not just a monkey, it is a monkey stung by a bee in its arse.

It seems almost impossible to concentrate and focus.

But, what if I told you, there are simple yogic techniques, which when performed clear up your mind of all the noise and clutter and bestow upon you laser sharp focus, instantly.

Well, that is what the book is all about.

First, tell me, does this sounds familiar?

We humans, are nosy little creatures.

We have this urge and innate need to know everything that is happening around us.

No matter how irrelevant it is to us, we will take inconsiderate risks to know it all, and then find a way and design a logical sequence in our minds which will conclude that everything happening out there is about us.

And, as if that wasn't enough, we will go out the way to amplify the negative aspects of it

and make our own lives difficult.

Can I get a "Oh, Yeah....!!!".

And as it is said '***Our thoughts create our reality***', these negative thoughts lead to an unfulfilling life, riddled with anxiety, stress and ill health.

The Ancient Indian Yogic techniques:

The Indian philosophy recorded in the Upanishads says that, *we are truly alive only in the 'present'*.

We can dwell on the past, dream of the future, but we get to 'Live' only the present.

Advait

It is the only thing in our control, that we can feel, experience and enjoy.

Here, the vedic philosophy introduces the concept of *atma-chitta,* being aware and mindful, the only way that can lead to a happy life.

But, when our mind is cluttered with negative thoughts and emotions, when we are hopping from one irrelevant thought to other, we simply lose the moment and basically forget to 'Live'.

Also, it affects every aspect of our lives;

If your mind is filled with chaotic thoughts, you won't be able to focus on the work at hand, thus adversely affecting your productivity and the quality of your work, this takes a toll on your professional life.

If you are not focused on what your partner is saying and don't pay keen attention to your communication, your relationship will take a hit.

In a similar way it will affect your family life, your friend circle, essentially, every human contact will be affected in the long run.

The more chaotic and crowded your mind becomes, the more anxious and stressed you get.

The Rishis, Seers and Yogis of ancient India had a similar problem to that we do now.

They were very intelligent men who sat, thought on complex matters and meditated continuously. How crowded and cluttered their minds may have been.

Although the meditation helped improve their minds, they realized that the more complex the matter they thought about, the harder it became to focus and concentrate.

As a result these thinking men developed a series of yogic techniques that decluttered their minds of irrelevant noise and distractions in just a few minutes.

They could be done anywhere, anytime in just a few minutes without working up a sweat.

They were the answer to their problem, and those techniques will be the answer for us easy living modern people.

I won't take any more of your time, let's get down to business.

How to use the techniques you will learn in this book?

I will teach you 15 Yogic techniques in this book, but I will also say this, you cannot expect to perform these exercises one time and then expect to have a decluttered mind forever.

These techniques are essentially micro-exercises, which will work wonders for you when you include them in your daily routine and cultivate them as 'habits'.

Based on the experiences of my clients and students, techniques #1 and #15 are the two most effective techniques.

Hence, practice those 2 techniques daily, and then pick and choose any 2-3 other techniques to go with them, so that you go through all the techniques at least once a week.

(Practice the techniques twice per day, once in the morning and then in the evening.)

Maintain your practice for 4 weeks and then you will find out by experience that a few techniques work really well for you more than the others. Then inculcate those techniques as 'habits' by practicing them every time you need to clear your mind and relax.

Mudras

(मुद्रा)

What are Mudras?

According to the Vedic culture of ancient India, our entire world is made of 'the five elements' called as *The Panch-Maha-Bhuta's*. The five elements being **Earth**, **Water**, **Fire**, **Wind** and **Space/Vacuum**. They are also called the earth element, water element, fire element, wind element and space element.

These five elements constitute the human body – the nutrients from the soil (earth) are absorbed by the plants which we consume (thus we survive on the earth element), the blood flowing through own veins represents the water element, the body heat represents the fire element, the oxygen we inhale and the carbon dioxide we exhale represents the wind element and the sinuses we have in our nose and skull represent the space element.

As long as these five elements in our body are balanced and maintain appropriate levels we remain healthy. An imbalance of these elements in the human body leads to a deteriorated health and diseases.

Now understand this, the command and control center of all these five elements lies in our fingers. So literally, our health lies at our fingertips.

The Mudra healing method that I am going to teach you depends on our fingers.

Advait

To understand this, we should first know the finger-element relationship:

Thumb – Fire element.

Index finger – Wind element.

Middle finger – Space/Vacuum element.

Third finger – Earth element.

Small finger – Water element.

This image will give you a better understanding of the concept:

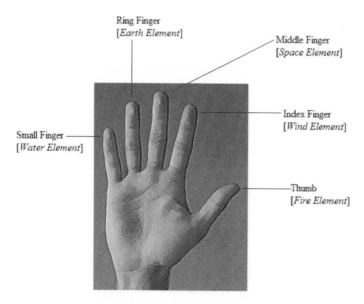

When the fingers are brought together in a specific pattern and are touched to each other, or slightly pressed against each other, the formation is called as a 'Mudra'.

When the five fingers are touched and pressed in a peculiar way to form a Mudra, it affects the levels of the five elements in our body, thus balancing those elements and inducing good health.

Important

For the better understanding of the reader, detail images have been provided for every mudra along with the method to perform it.

The Mudras whose images show only one hand performing the Mudra, are to be performed simultaneously on both your hands for the Mudras to have the maximum effect.

Also, if you want to learn more about Mudras, you can grab my **FREE** book,

"Mudras for Beginner's" here:

https://www.amazon.com/dp/B00XWCR26I

Technique #1

Shankhvartamudra / Mudra of Conch II

Method:

This Mudra has to be performed in a seated position.

Advait

Be seated comfortably in an upright posture and concentrate on your breathing to relax.

Hold your palms in front of your chest facing each other.

Now extend all the fingers on both the hands outwards.

Then, touch the tips of all the fingers of one hand to the tips of the respective fingers of the other hand.

Then bend the right Index finger at an angle of 90 degrees at the second knuckle. (Refer the image)

Hold this Mudra in front of your chest.

Focus your eyes on the tip of your middle fingers and concentrate on your breathing.

Duration:

This Mudra should be performed for at least 7 minutes and can be performed for 40 minutes at a stretch.

Other Benefits:

- This Mudra is known to sharpen and strengthen your intuition.

- Many practitioners also say that this Mudra helps them to connect you to your 'inner self'.

- It also helps in reducing anxiety.

Note:

I dare you, no matter how hard you try, you will not be able to consciously distract yourself with irrelevant thoughts while performing this Mudra.

See for yourself.

Technique #2

Dnyaanmudra / Mudra of Knowledge (Wisdom)

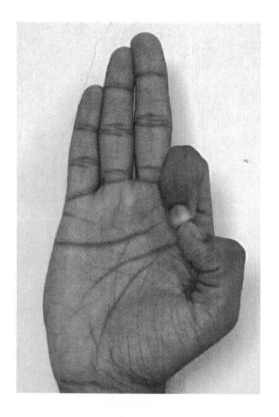

Method:

This Mudra has to be performed in a seated position.

Be seated comfortably in an upright posture and concentrate on your breathing to relax.

Join the tips of your Index finger and Thumb together and press slightly.

Keep all the other fingers extended outwards as shown in the image.

After forming the Mudras on both the hands, rest the Mudras on your thighs, palms facing up.

Duration:

This Mudra should be performed for at least 5 minutes and can be performed for 20 minutes at a stretch.

Other Benefits:

- This Mudra also helps in strengthening your respiratory system.

- It is extremely useful in increasing ones *'Prana'* energy and focusing it inwards.

Technique #3

Panchmukhmudra / Mudra of Five Faces

Method:

This Mudra has to be performed in a seated position.

Be seated comfortably in an upright posture and concentrate on your breathing to relax.

Hold your palms in front of your chest facing each other.

Now extend all the fingers on both the hands outwards.

Then, touch tips of all fingers of one hand to the tips of the respective fingers of the other hand. (refer the image)

Press the tips slightly.

Once the Mudra is formed lower the Mudra hold it in front of your abdomen.

Duration:

This Mudra should be performed for at least 5 minutes and can be performed for 20 minutes at a stretch.

Other Benefits:

- This Mudra strengthens your bodies self-healing mechanism.

- It is also very helpful in maintaining the health of your tendons and ligaments.

- It helps in improving your memory.

Technique #4

Dvimukhamudra / Mudra of Two Faces

Method:

This Mudra has to be performed in a seated position.

Be seated comfortably in an upright posture and concentrate on your breathing to relax.

Hold your palms in front of your chest facing you.

Now extend all the fingers on both the hands outwards.

Then, touch tips of the Little finger and Ring finger of one hand to the tips of the Little finger and Ring finger of the other hand and press slightly. (refer the image)

Once the Mudra is formed lower the Mudra hold it in front of your abdomen.

Duration:

This Mudra should be performed for at least 5 minutes and can be performed for 40 minutes at a stretch.

Other Benefits:

- This Mudra balances the water element and the earth element in your body.

- It is also very helpful in curing digestive disorders.

- It helps in maintaining your kidneys healthy.

Technique #5

Kaaleshwarmudra / Mudra of the Lord of Time

Method:

This Mudra has to be performed in a seated position.

Be seated comfortably in an upright posture and concentrate on your breathing to relax.

Touch the tip of the middle finger of your left hand with the tip of the middle finger of your right hand.

Touch the tip of the thumb of your left hand with the tip of the thumb of your right hand.

Keep the middle fingers and thumbs stretched and straight.

Bend the other fingers and let them touch each other at the joints, as shown in the image.

Hold this Mudra in front of your chest.

Duration:

This Mudra should be performed for at least 5 minutes and can be performed for 30 minutes at a stretch.

Other Benefits:

- This Mudra is really effective in getting rid of addictions.

- It is also very helpful in strengthening the heart muscles.

- It also maintains the health of your brain.

Pranayama

(प्राणायाम)

Advait

What is Pranayama?

Pranayama is considered of paramount importance in Yoga.

The word Pranayama is made of two basic Sanskrit words-

Pran (पूराण) = Life or Universal Life Energy.

Ayam (आयाम) = to Extend and Elongate.

Thus Pranayama means 'an exercise which is to be performed if you want to extend your life'.

Pranayama is the fuel of life...

Here is an interesting analogy-

You are familiar with the existence of the seven (7) chakras along the spine,

which are considered as the energy points sustaining life and health.

If these Chakras are the rotating wind mills which produce energy to sustain life,

then prana is the essential wind energy which makes the hands of a wind mill rotate, to produce that energy.

When we breathe in we take in the essential oxygen along with the all-pervading Prana.

[And when we breath out we push out the expended energy and toxins out of our body.]

Ayurveda calls our digestion as 'Jathar Agni' literally meaning 'digestive fire', it compares our digestive process with a 'Yadnya' - A holy Pyre, where things are offered to the gods.

And the 'Prana' we take in, is the fuel for this holy Yadnya.

When we practice Pranayama, we regulate and streamline the process of drawing in the universal life force and thus enhancing our health and longevity.

This is the metaphysical Prana aspect of it.

Now let us look at the physical significance, but for that I first need to tell you about our bodies' digestive and excretory mechanism.

We consume food, which is broken down into small pieces by our teeth and is added primary digestive enzymes from the saliva in our mouth.

It then passes into our stomach, where it is churned and more gastric juices are added to it to induce breakdown of the food consumed.

This mixture then passes through our intestines, whose walls absorb the nutrients from the food and deposit them into the blood stream to be taken all around the body.

The blood when passing through the lungs also absorbs oxygen that we have inhaled.

So the blood carries the nutrients and the oxygen essential for the cells in our body to break down the nutrients into packets of energy.

Thus the cells of our body get nutrients and oxygen from blood, break down the nutrients into energy and Life is Sustained!!!

But like any other mechanism in this universe, every step produces a byproduct in form of waste.

The food post-digestion in excreted form the intestines in form of stool.

Impurities in our blood are separated in our kidneys and excreted in form of urine.

The impurities/toxins created at the cellular level are in two forms, liquid and volatile.

The liquid toxins are put out by our skin in form of sweat. (You will be surprised to know that our skin is the largest excretory organ in our body)

The volatile toxins (which are most harmful) are thrown out in form of toxic gases using our lungs, when we BREATHE OUT!!!

Pranayama plays a pivotal role here in ridding our bodies of these harmful toxins.

It supplies our lungs and hence our blood with abundant supply of fresh oxygen.

It boosts our immune system.

It is amazingly effective in calming down your mind.

It helps in improving our memory, virility and strengthens our neurological system.

There are many other Pranayama techniques which can be used for multiple other purposes, if you want to learn more about those Pranayama techniques, you can grab my bestselling book;

"Pranayama: The Vedic Science of Breath" here;

https://www.amazon.com/dp/B075KPDP7H

Technique #6

Bhramari Pranayama/Pranayama of the Hornet

Method:

Sit in Sukhasan.

Close your eyes.

Then close your ears with your thumbs, place your index fingers on your forehead, and place the remaining three fingers on your eyes and press the ridge between your eyes slightly with your middle finger.

Inhale to your full capacity; hold the breath in for a couple of seconds.

Then keeping your mouth closed, exhale slowly while making the 'Aum' sound (Om Chant).

(This step creates a sound similar to the buzzing of a hornet's wings hence the name.)

Duration:

No specific duration. Repeat it for at least 2-3 times.

Other Benefits:

-This Pranayama is extremely essential for maintaining the health of your throat and thyroid.

-It cures any hoarseness of voice caused by any illness.

-Regular practice of this Pranayama increases your concentration and also calms your mind.

-You'll feel a soothing peace and calmness when you perform this Pranayama regularly.

Technique #7

Kapaalbhati Pranayama/Pranayama for forehead cleanse

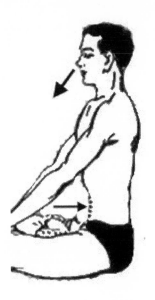

Method:

Sit in Sukhasan and form the dnyanamudra with your hands and place them on your knees with your palms facing upwards.

Close your eyes.

Advait

Then, exhale quickly in a single stroke/movement. Your lungs will contract in that moment and your stomach will be sucked in.

Don't inhale purposefully; once you exhale rapidly inhaling will happen as a reflex.

Keep repeating the exhaling action and with every breath that comes out visualize every impurity within, every toxic matter and each negative thought is being thrown out of your body.

Caution:

- People suffering from back pain and waist pain should perform the exhaling motion a bit slowly.

- People suffering with Heart diseases should perform the exhaling motion slowly.

- Pregnant women should NOT practice this Pranayama.

Duration:

Practice this Pranayama for 4-5 minutes in the start, but with regular practice gradually increase the duration to 12-15 minutes. (If at the start you feel tired after a few minutes, stop for a few seconds and then continue again.)

Other Benefits:

You will be amazed with the benefits of this Pranayama:

-It is very helpful in burning excess fat.

-It is very helpful in regulating your blood sugar levels and thus keeps diabetes in check.

-It is found to be very effective in clearing heart blockages in people suffering from arteriosclerosis. (but please perform the exhaling motion slowly)

-It maintains the health of your liver.

-It helps in getting rid of constipation.

-It is even observed that a regular practice of this Pranayama cures Hepatitis.

-It reduces the amount of phlegm in your body and is also very helpful for patients suffering from Asthma.

-It is very helpful for people suffering from pollen and dust allergies.

-It is observed that a regular practice of this Pranayama reduces the size of Tumors and cysts in the body. (There have been many cases where patients have reported that their tumors have completely dissolved due to a regular and disciplined practice of this Pranayama.)

-In women it is found to cure any uterine ailments.

-It is even found to be extremely effective in curing skin diseases.

-It is very effective in curing diseases of the throat.

-It brings a peculiar glow to the aura of the practitioner.

Technique #8

Relaxing Breath

Method:

- Lie on a mat, facing up.

- Your head, neck, spine and legs should be aligned in a straight line. Your heels should be touching each other.

- Place your hands at your side palms facing down.

- Now slowly start breathing. See to it that the breath is so slow and steady that it does not make any sound.

- After you have taken a few breaths, practice equal breathing. (Equal breathing is when the duration for inhaling, holding the breath in and exhaling is the same.)

- If you inhale for 10 seconds, hold the breath in for 10 seconds and exhale in 10 seconds, all without making any gushing sound.

- Remain in this position for 3-4 min., but if you find it particularly relaxing, you can practice it for as long as you want.

Other Benefits:

- As the name suggests, it is extremely relaxing.

- It is very helpful in increasing one's ability to focus and concentrate.

Yoga Asanas

(योगासन)

Advait

The True Meaning of Yoga

There is a common and popular belief that 'Yoga' is an Indian ritual which is all about performing difficult physical exercises for maintaining health and curing diseases.

This is a MYTH!!

Actually, sound health is a side-effect of Yoga.

Surprising!!! But true.

The word 'Yoga' literally means *to unite ourselves with our higher self* - an entirely meta-physical objective which can be achieved through a Discipline of Physical exercises (Asana's) coupled with Meditation exercises (*Dhyana*) and Breathing exercises (Pranayam). When we perform those exercises we get in shape and achieve good health.

Yoga is not something which is only to be performed or practiced; it is also to be achieved.

Yoga is the destination and the path to it is through a disciplined practice of physical exercises, meditation and breathing exercises.

Maharshi Patanjali, in his revolutionary work *'Paatanjal YogaSutra'* prescribes an eight-fold path to achieve Yoga, known as *Ashtang Yoga.*

['Paatanjal YogaSutra' is considered to be the most comprehensive book on Yoga and it forms the basis and reference of all the Yoga methodologies practiced throughout the world today.]

The Ashtang Yoga [eight-fold path to yoga], given by Maharshi Patanjali is as follows:

Yama

The moral virtues that one should possess as they are considered to be essential for one's initiation on the path to yoga.

Niyama

It involves being knowledgeable and aware about your surroundings and then studying your-self to form an essential discipline which you would adhere to.

Asana

'Understanding and Performing' the required physical exercises, this is the core of your yoga practice.

Advait

Pranayama

It is all about breath control, which enhances the life energy which governs the existence of a being and balances the mental energy.

Pratyahar

Sensory inhibitions which internalize the consciousness and prepare your mind to take action.

Dharana

It involves inculcating an extended mental focus to concentrate on only those things that are essential.

Dhyana

It involves meditation, paying attention to your breathing and thus focusing only on yourself.

Samadhi

Becoming one with the object of your contemplation and experiencing spiritual liberation.

Yama and Niyama are essential for inculcating the needed discipline and to establish a strict routine.

Asana is the crucial physical part, which subjects your body to essential physical movements through different exercises.

Pranayam and Pratyahar are needed to guide us through the various breathing exercises and for making us aware of the internal spiritual changes as we ascend along the path to Yoga.

Dharana and Dhyana stages prepare us mentally and spiritually to concentrate inwards by using various meditation exercises.

Samadhi is the culmination stage where one achieves Yoga.

Technique #9

Dhruv Asan/Asana of Dhruv Rishi

Method:

Stand straight on the mat with your feet together.

Lift your right leg up and pull it up with your hands and place the heel of your right feet on the inner side of your left thigh.

Now, join your hands together palm-to-palm to form the *Namaste* gesture.

Remain in this position for a few seconds and then return to the normal standing position.

Repeat the Asana with the other leg.

(Initially you may not be able to balance yourself, so instead of doing the Namaste gesture, you can use your hands to get support from a steady object.)

Duration:

This Asana takes 12-15 seconds to perform and you can repeat it 2-3 times.

Other Benefits:

-It strengthens your ankles and knees.

-It helps in increasing your balance.

-Its regular practice increases your focus and concentration.

-Its regular practice also strengthens your respiratory system.

Advait

Technique #10

Trikon Asan/Asana of the Triangle

Method:

Stand straight on the mat with your feet shoulder length apart.

Lift your right hand up while keeping your left hand at your side, touching your thigh.

Now, bend your body to your left and slide your left hand down, along your left leg.

(do all this without bending your knees)

Remain in this position for a few seconds and then return to the normal standing position.

Repeat the Asana but on the other side. [i.e. lift up your left hand and bend towards your right while sliding your right hand along your right leg.]

Duration:

This Asana takes 12-15 seconds to perform and you can repeat it 4-5 times.

Other Benefits:

-It strengthens your hips, hamstrings and thighs.

-It helps in regulating blood pressure.

-Its regular practice increases your focus and concentration.

-Its regular practice is very helpful in maintain a calm composure.

-It also helps in improving your balance.

Technique #11

Tiryak Bhujang Asan/Asana of the Twisting Snake

Method:

Lie down on the mat/ground facing down, i.e. your stomach, chest and chin touching the ground, with your hands at your side, palms facing down.

Then, placing your palms adjacent to your respective shoulders, push your upper torso up. (Refer Image)

Your groin should still be touching the ground.

Then slowly inhaling, turn your upper torso to your right, as much as you comfortably can.

Hold this position for a few seconds and then return back to the initial lying down position, while exhaling slowly.

Repeat the process, but this time turn your upper torso to your left.

This will complete one set of this Asana.

Duration:

Repeat at least 2-3 sets of this Asana.

Other Benefits:

-This Asana enhances strength of your upper back.

-Regular practice of this Asana cures cervical spondylitis and helps prevent it.

-It opens up your chest muscles and also strengthens your lungs.

-Its regular practice helps in toning internal organs in your upper torso.

-It helps in regulating blood sugar levels.

-Regular practice of this Asana improves your memory and concentration.

Meditation

(ध्यान)

Technique #12

Nature Meditation

(Practice it when the sky isn't too bright, so not at high noon, either early in morning or towards evening)

- This is an open-eyed meditation, done standing up.

- Go on a rooftop or an open ground from where you have a good look at the sky.

- Stand up straight, with your feet spread shoulder length apart.

- Start breathing slightly deeper than normal.

- Concentrate on your breath for 1-2 minutes.

- Now spread out your hands wide, palms facing up and look up at the sky.

- Look at the clear sky above without blinking.

- Do not blink at all and look at a single point in the sky.

- You will notice that once you stop the movement of your eyes (blinking as well as eye-ball movement), all the thoughts stop and there is nothing but silence within the mind and peace.

- Remain in this state for as long you feel comfortable.

Technique #13

Thought Meditation

(Though we are practicing these techniques for decluttering the mind, this particular meditation floods your mind with thoughts and then inculcates in the practitioner a habit of being neutral and unnerved by any thought that occurs and to clear out your mind with a single deep breath.)

Method:

Sit in Sukhasan and form the dnyanamudra (technique #2) with your hands and place them on your knees with your palms facing upwards.

(If you cannot sit down with folded legs, sit in a chair, with your feet flat on the ground and with a straight back)

Close your eyes and maintain a normal pace of breathing.

Concentrate on your breath and be aware and mindful of the air you inhale and exhale.

Remain in this state for a minute or two.

Then ask yourself this question, 'Who Am I?'

Let the answers flow into your mind.

Don't think about the answers, don't contemplate on them, just be there and be a witness to the answers that come to your mind.

Remain in this state for a minute and then take a deep breath in, and as you exhale out, visualize all the answers that came to you, being shoved out of your mind along with your breath.

Then ask yourself the second question, 'What Do I Want?'

Let the answers flood in, just 'be' there.

And then do the deep breath and the long exhale.

Then move onto the third question, 'What is My Purpose Here?'

Let the answers flood in, just 'be' there.

And then do the deep breath and the long exhale.

Now, concentrate on your breath and be aware and mindful of the air you inhale and exhale.

Remain in this state for a minute and then slowly open your eyes.

Technique #14

'Aum' Meditation

Method:

Sit in Sukhasan and form the dnyanamudra (technique #2) with your hands and place them on your knees with your palms facing upwards.

(If you cannot sit down with folded legs, sit in a chair, with your feet flat on the ground and with a straight back)

Close your eyes and behind closed eyelids, focus your eyes at the midpoint between your eye-brows.

Then deeply inhale through your nose.

First fill the air in your lungs and then into your belly.

Hold the air in for a few seconds, and then slowly exhale through your mouth chanting 'Aum'.

Practice this meditation for 4-5 minutes.

Mantra

(मंत्र)

Technique #15

Gayatri Mantra

To be honest, to explain the Gayatri Mantra to you and about its importance in Indian spirituality and philosophy will require a book of its own.

Here, I will only tell you what the Mantra is, a rough superficial meaning and how to pronounce it with help of a mp3 recording done in my own voice.

The Gayatri Mantra:

Aum
Bhur
Bhuva-Svaha

Tat
Savitur
Varenyam

Bhargo
Devasya
Dhee-Mahi

Dhiyo
Yo-Naha

Pracho-Dayaat

Advait

Meaning of the Mantra:

Gayatri mantra = *a prayer to the Divine light.*

"We meditate on that most adored Supreme Lord, the creator,

whose divine light illumines all realms (physical, mental and spiritual).

May this divine light illumine our intellect."

Download the audio recording here:

https://goo.gl/9gDrxX

Sit in Sukhasan and form the dnyanamudra (technique #2) with your hands and place them on your knees with your palms facing upwards.

(If you cannot sit down with folded legs, sit in a chair, with your feet flat on the ground and with a straight back)

Close your eyes and behind closed eyelids, focus your eyes at the midpoint between your eye-brows.

Now recite the Mantra for 3-4 minutes.

(chant along with the audio recording till you learn the mantra and are able to say it yourself)

Thank You!

Thank you so much for reading my book. I hope you really liked it.

As you probably know, many people look at the reviews on Amazon before they decide to purchase a book.

If you liked the book, please take a minute to leave a review with your feedback.

60 seconds is all I'm asking for, and it would mean a lot to me.

Thank You so much.

All the best,

Advait

Other Books by Advait

On Mudra Healing

Mudras for Awakening Chakras: 19 Simple Hand
Gestures for Awakening & Balancing Your Chakras

http://www.amazon.com/dp/B00P82COAY

[#1 Bestseller in 'Yoga']

[#1 Bestseller in 'Chakras']

Mudras for Weight Loss: 21 Simple Hand Gestures for Effortless Weight Loss

http://www.amazon.com/dp/B00P3ZPSEK

Advait

Mudras for Spiritual Healing: 21 Simple Hand
Gestures for Ultimate Spiritual Healing & Awakening

http://www.amazon.com/dp/B00PFYZLQO

Mudras for Sex: 25 Simple Hand Gestures for
Extreme Erotic Pleasure & Sexual Vitality

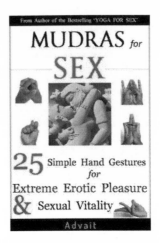

<u>http://www.amazon.com/dp/B00OJR1DRY</u>

Advait

Mudras: 25 Ultimate Techniques for Self Healing

http://www.amazon.com/dp/B00MMPB5CI

Mudras of Anxiety: 25 Simple Hand Gestures for Curing Anxiety

http://www.amazon.com/dp/B00PF011IU

Advait

Mudras for a Strong Heart: 21 Simple Hand Gestures
for Preventing, Curing & Reversing Heart Disease

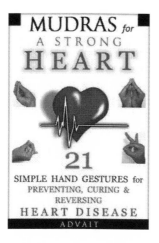

http://www.amazon.com/dp/B00PFRLGTM

Mudras for Curing Cancer: 21 Simple Hand Gestures
for Preventing & Curing Cancer

http://www.amazon.com/dp/B00PFO199M

Advait

Mudras for Stress Management: 21 Simple Hand
Gestures for a Stress Free Life

http://amazon.com/dp/BooPFTJ6OC

Mudras for Memory Improvement: 25 Simple Hand
Gestures for Ultimate Memory Improvement

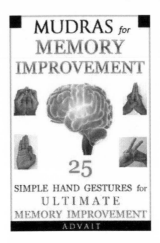

http://www.amazon.com/dp/B00PFSP8TK

Advait

On Yoga

Easy Yoga: Your Ultimate Beginners Guide to Understanding Yoga and Leading a Disease-Free Life through Routine Yoga Practice

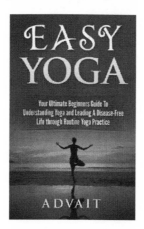

http://www.amazon.com/dp/B010I97366

Monday Yoga: Pranayam and Sukshma-Asana's for starting Your Routine Yoga Practice and Inducing Vigor into Your Life on the first day of the Week

http://www.amazon.com/dp/B011SI6MK4

Tuesday Yoga: 12 Yoga Asanas to be performed on
Tuesday as a Part of Your Daily Yoga Routine

http://www.amazon.com/dp/B013GGA1AS

Wednesday Yoga: 12 Yoga Asanas to be performed on Wednesday as a Part of Your Daily Yoga Routine

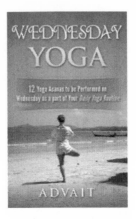

http://www.amazon.com/dp/B014RTDQ5U

Advait

Thursday Yoga: 12 Yoga Asanas to be performed on
Thursday as a Part of Your Daily Yoga Routine

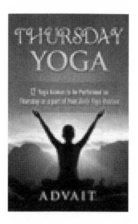

http://www.amazon.com/dp/B015JMSEPQ

Friday Yoga: 12 Yoga Asanas to be performed on Friday as a Part of Your Daily Yoga Routine

http://www.amazon.com/dp/B015UK17KG

Advait

Saturday Yoga: 12 Yoga Asanas to be performed on Saturday as a Part of Your Daily Yoga Routine

http://www.amazon.com/dp/B0165WFUJW

Sunday Yoga: Suryanamaskar (Sun Salutation) & 5 Yoga Asanas for a Blissful Culmination of Your Daily Yoga Routine

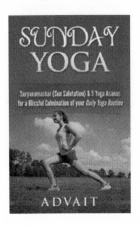

http://www.amazon.com/dp/B016Q8GF8K

Book Excerpt

Advait

7 Days to a Stress-Free Life

Ultimate Vedic Guide to using Mudras, Yoga & Ayurveda for Busting Stress, Training your Body to remain Calm and have a Relaxed Mind all the time.

by

Advait

Content

Stress – The Modern Day Pandemic

If you are familiar with my previous works, you know that I like to keep all my books fluff-free and concise. This one won't be any different.

I will not waste 20 pages on educating you about the definitions of Stress, rather I would like you to tell you how stress affects us.

To understand the severity of stress, you guys have to first understand how our body's immunity mechanism works.

Located just above our heart is a small grey gland, nestled securely behind the breastbone, called as the Thymus gland.

Our body's immune system depends directly on the health of our Thymus gland.

This gland produces millions-n-millions of lymphocytes each day.

These lymphocytes are like millions of Clark Kents patrolling all around within our body, and when they encounter murderous toxins, parasites and bacteria, these Clark Kents throw away their dorky glasses, tear out their shirts and transform into Superman a.k.a.

Macrophages, that eradicate all these toxins and harmful parasites, thus maintaining our health.

There is another gland in our body, called as the Adrenal gland.

It is the primary gland in our body that reacts to external stress.

When you are under stress, your adrenal gland produces a steroid called Cortisol.

This Cortisol is the Cryptonite to our Clark Kents.

The Lymphocytes in our body become useless in presence of Cortisol, hence they cannot fight off the toxins, bacteria and external parasites. Thus our immune system fails us and we fall ill.

Hence those people who are often under stress regularly struggle with cold and flu.

How long term stress affects our personal health:

Heart-

The first organ of our body that stress affects is the heart.

Every time we are stressed we are putting unnecessary pressure on our cardiovascular system, which in turn affects our blood pressure.

Also, recent studies have shown that increased stress induces blood clotting within our blood vessels and these miniscule clots build up into larger ones owing to prolonged stress over time and can lead to a stroke.

Such pressures on ones circulatory system over a prolonged period increase the chances of a heart attack.

(Shocking fact: 3 people die in America every 2 min. from a heart disease).

Immune System-

As I have already told you, stress directly suppresses your immune system.

What is more dangerous is the increased probability to fall prey to Cancer due to a faulty immune system.

A recent study shows that 1 of every 2 men had a risk of developing Cancer in their lifetime and this risk factor increases manifolds when you add stress to the scenario.

Digestive System:

Prolonged stress adversely effects your digestive system. It suppresses its effectiveness thus slowing down your metabolism.

Selective appetite goes up (stress eating) but at the same time your metabolism slows down drastically which results in excess consumption of unwanted calories leading to complexities like obesity, hypertension etc.

Blood Sugar Level:

Whenever you are under stress your blood sugar level spikes up. This phenomenon over a longer period owing to prolonged stress will lead to diabetes, obesity, kidney failure and other renal disorders.

Rapid aging:

If one is regularly under stress, studies show that the human body gradually decreases the secretion of anti-aging growth hormones, which can lead to premature aging.

Libido:

Stress reduces the secretion of our sex hormones, thus adversely affecting our libido and sex drive.

This might have an adverse effect on our relationships in the short-term, but in the long term it can cause sexual dysfunction and infertility.

Depression and Dementia:

Studies have shown that if you have high secretion of cortisol over a longer period of time it can cause insomnia, anxiety, depression and in severe cases can lead to Alzheimer's disease and dementia.

The Most Common Remedies and their Side-Effects:

The most common medications used are anti-depressants and sleep inducing sedatives. They come with immediate effects and relief, but it is a temporary solution, effective only for a short-term, addictive and come with a baggage of health hazards.

Here are some potential threats you are exposed to if you consume these type of medications:

- Headaches, allergic reactions and blurred vision.

- Impaired driving is one of the biggest problems with sedatives; people don't realize they're still hazy and it is like driving drunk thus increasing the risk of accidents drastically.

- They don't go well with other medicines, i.e. if you are on some medications and you also consume these pills you can't anticipate how this combination might hit you.

- Prolonged consumption can cause sexual dysfunction.

- They cause drastic weight fluctuations.

- They cause internal electrolytic imbalance.

- They are extremely addictive and if you form a habit you'll end up being worse off when you decide to stop consuming them, because your body will then be adapted to them—and that means you'll have more difficulty coping with stress naturally.

The Full-Proof, No Side-Effects solution for a Stress-Free life – Vedic Healing:

Mudra healing, Yoga and Ayurveda are the 3 pillars of the Vedic healing system which forms the base of '7 Days to a Stress-Free Life'.

Each day of this system comprises of;

3 Mudras,

2 Pranayam Asanas,

3 Yoga Asanas and

2 Ayurvedic Serums,

Which help you lead a stress-free life instantly and without any side-effects.

Advait

Day 1

Step #1

Bhastrika Pranayama/Pranayama of Bellow

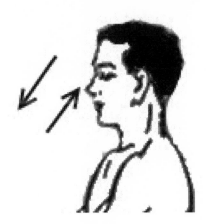

Method:

Sit in Sukhasana and form the dnyanamudra with your hands and place them on your knees with your palms facing upwards.

('Dnyanamudra' is formed when you join the tips of your index finger and your thumb while keeping your other fingers outstretched.)

Close your eyes.

Inhale to your full capacity; hold the breath in for a couple of seconds and then exhale slowly.

When you inhale, fill the air into your lungs and expand your chest while inhaling and it will press your diaphragm down;

Do not expand your stomach while inhaling.

Concentrate completely on your breathing and pay attention to how you feel with every breath you take.

Visualize, every breath nourishing all the parts of your body.

Duration:

Perform this Pranayama for at least 3 minutes.

Other Benefits:

-This is a nourishing exercise and it enhances your digestive capabilities and creates heat in the body.

-It helps in burning the excess fat.

-It helps in reducing the amount of phlegm.

-It is very effective in cases of Asthma.

-It strengthens your Lungs.

-It helps in purifying blood and facilitates efficient blood circulation.

Step #2

Detox Breath I

Method:

- Stand up without slouching and with your back straight.

- Keep a space of 10-12 inches between your feet.

- See to it that your body weight is equally distributed on both your feet.

- Put out your chest, keep your neck straight and slightly pull down your chin.

- Keep your hands at your sides with your palms touching your thighs.

- Now, slowly but steadily take in a deep breath.

- First fill in your chest with air, once the chest is full then, fill the air in your belly.

- Hold the air in for as long as you comfortably can.

- Then open your mouth and rapidly exhale through your mouth by contracting your stomach but keeping your chest rigid.

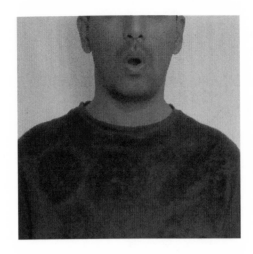

- This completes one practice of this Pranayama.

- Perform 8-10 repetitions.

- Take a rest of 1-2 min. before doing anything else.

Other Benefits:

-This Pranayama is especially effective in pushing the volatile toxins from the lungs and the stomach out of the body

-Also, this breath rejuvenates the organs in the chest cavity and neck.

Step #3

Samputamudra / Mudra of Bud

Method:

It's a modified form of the 'Prayer Mudra'.

This Mudra is to be performed in a seated position.

Be seated comfortably in an upright posture and concentrate on your breathing to relax.

Touch the tip of the fingers of your right hand with the tip of the fingers of your left hand as shown in the image.

Make hollow space between both the palms as if you are holding a small bird.

Now, take this formation in front of your eyes, and look through the hollow space and concentrate on your breathing for a couple of minutes, then hold this Mudra in front of your Heart.

Duration:

This Mudra should be performed for at least 5 minutes and can be performed for 30 minutes at a stretch.

This Mudra should be performed twice a day, once in the morning and once in the evening for best results.

Step #4

Swastikasan/Asana of Swastika

The Sanskrit word *Swastika* means pious. (do not confuse a swastika with the 'nazi symbol' which is an 'inverted' swastik)

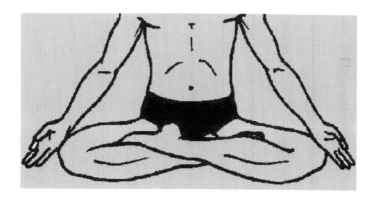

Method:

Sit comfortably on the mat.

Sit straight, with your spine erect. Do not slouch over.

Now fold your legs is such a way that the toes of your right foot are pressed between the thigh and calf muscle of the left leg and the toes of your left foot are pressed between the thigh and calf muscle of the right leg. (refer image)

Rest your hands on your knees, with your palms facing upwards.

Touch the tip of the index finger to the tip of the thumb on both your hands. (this hand gesture is called a 'Dnyanmudra')

Keep breathing slowly and comfortably while you perform this Asana.

Duration:

This Asana (position) should be held for 2-3 minutes.

Repeat at least 3 times for best results.

Other Benefits:

-This Asana enhances mental strength

-It helps in calming down your mind.

-It strengthens your nervous system.

-On the physical front, This Asana helps in keeping Diabetes under control.

-It also strengthens the Pancreas.

Step #5

Tritiiya Varahamudra / Mudra of Hog III

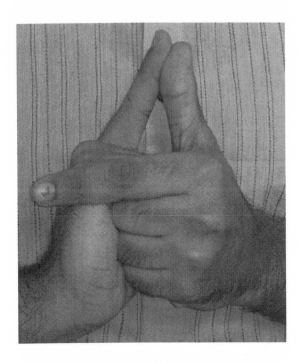

Method:

This Mudra is to be performed in a seated position.

Be seated comfortably in an upright posture and concentrate on your breathing to relax.

Hold your left hand in front of your chest, palm facing you.

Curl the Middle, Ring and Little finger of the left hand inwards.

The Index finger should be pointing towards right and the Thumb should be extended upwards.

Now, clasp the curled fingers of the left hand with the fingers of the right hand.

Then, touch the tip of the Thumb of your left hand with the tip of the Index finger of your right hand.

Touch the tip of your right Thumb to the base of the left Thumb.

The Left Index finger should be resting outside the right Little finger.

Duration:

This Mudra should be performed for at least 5 minutes and can be performed for 45 minutes at a stretch.

This Mudra should be performed twice a day, once in the morning and once in the evening for best results.

Step #6

Padmasan/ Asana of Lotus

Method:

Sit comfortably on the mat with your legs stretched out front.

Now, fold your right leg and place the foot on your left thigh with the base of the right foot (palm of the foot) facing upwards. (refer the image)

Then, fold your left leg and place the foot on your right thigh with the base of the left foot (palm of the foot) facing upwards.

The heel of both your feet should be touching the base of the opposite thighs.

Rest your hands on your knees, with your palms facing upwards.

Touch the tip of the Index finger to the tip of the Thumb on both your hands.

Keep breathing slowly and comfortably while you perform this Asana.

(You will feel some pain when you are just starting out but with 4-5 days of regular practice, you should feel no discomfort.)

Duration:

When you perform this Asana for the first few days, do it only for 8-10 seconds at a stretch. But, with practice you'll fell more supple and flexible and then perform it for 1-2 minutes at a stretch.

Other Benefits:

-It works miraculously well in treating Arthritis.

- It enhances your digestive capabilities.

- It cures any stomach aches you have and increase hunger.

-It strengthens your heart.

-It imparts flexibility to all the organs below the waistline.

-Regular practice of this Asana induces mental & spiritual calmness.

Step #7

Dwitiiya Uttarbodhimudra / Mudra of Supreme Awakening II

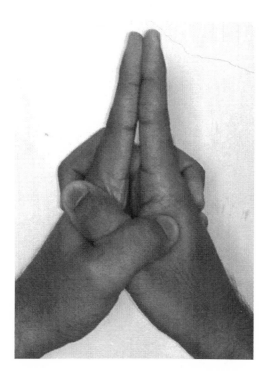

Method:

This Mudra is to be performed in a seated position.

Be seated comfortably in an upright posture and concentrate on your breathing to relax.

Clasp your hands together, and interlace the fingers of both the hands together.

Now join the tips of the Index finger as shown in the image and extend the Index fingers as upwards as possible,

Then cross-over the left Thumb on the right Thumb.

(Refer the image)

Duration:

This Mudra should be performed for at least 5 minutes and can be performed for 40 minutes at a stretch.

This Mudra should be performed twice a day, once in the morning and once in the evening for best results.

Step #8

Shavasana / Asana of Corpse

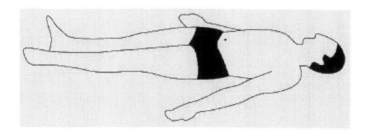

Method:

Lie down on the mat. Relax your body and bring your feet together, such that they are touching each other adjacently.

Keep your hands by your back with your palms facing upwards.

Close your eyes and breathe calmly for 10-12 seconds.

Then imagine/visualize a luminous beam of light entering your body through the top of your head and running along your spine and illuminating it.

Imagine the light entering your neck and nourishing your thyroid, and then imagine it entering your heart and bringing you more calmness.

Then imagine this light, spreading through your shoulders to your elbows and then onto your palms and then reaching and nourishing each and every finger of yours and then feel them getting relaxed completely.

Then this light overflows from your heart and fills all your chest cavity and abdomen, nourishing each and every organ in the abdomen and relaxing those organs.

Then this light, from the lower end of your spine, spreads into your hips and then flows into your legs and reaches every finger of your feet and internally nourishes them and then feel the entire lower part of your body very relaxed.

In the final phase, this light enters your face through your neck and nourishes your teeth, tongue, lips, nose, ears and eyes and then you feel those parts relaxed completely.

Keep breathing slowly and gently allow your breath to relax you more and more.

After about 10-12 minutes in this state, slowly roll to your right side while keeping your eyes closed. Stay in this state for a minute.

Then with the support of your right hand, sit up with your legs folded with eyes still closed.

Now breathe deeply, become aware of the environment around you and slowly open your eyes.

Duration:

This Asana takes around 15 minutes to perform.

Ayurvedic Breakfast Serum

Sweetened Cardamom Milk

Ingredients:

1 cup of Milk

1 ½ tbspn of Honey

2 pinches of Cardamom powder.

Instructions:

Bring the milk to a boil.

Turn off the heat and add honey and cardamom powder.

Stir well and consume while hot.

Ayurvedic Bedtime Serum

Ojas Peya (I)

Ingredients:

1 ½ cup of Milk

7-8 Almonds, soaked in water for 8/9 hours and finely chopped. (instead of soaked almonds you can also use blanched almonds in case you forget to soak them.)

5-6 Dates, deseeded and finely chopped

½ tspn of Cinnamon powder

½ tspn of Cardamom powder

¼ tspn of Turmeric powder

¼ tspn of Nutmeg powder

1 ½ tbspn of Ghee (Clarified Butter)

2-3 Black Peppercorns (crushed)

Instructions:

Add all the ingredients to the milk and stir thoroughly till the spice powders are mixed well.

Put this mixture in a blender to get thick consistency for the mixture.

After blending bring this mixture to a boil and then let it simmer for 2-3 minutes.

Turn off the heat.

Add Honey if you need it to be more sweet.

Consume while it is hot.

Pre-Sleep Breathing Routine

Lie in your bed, facing upwards with your eyes closed.

Both your hands should be by your side, adjacent to your thighs and palms facing upwards.

Inhale deeply but slowly and then exhale out the same way. Concentrate on your breathing for a couple of minutes.

Then, turn to your left (i.e. lie on your left side) and place your palms on your thighs.

Inhale in 3 installments, i.e, take 3 breaths, one followed by the other to fill your lungs. (do not exhale.)

Hold the breath in, as long as you can. Then exhale out slowly.

Repeat inhale-exhale pattern for 7-10 times.

Schedule for the Day

Morning:-

- Practice Step #1 through Step #8

Wait for 25-30 mins to eat your breakfast, make sure to end your breakfast with the *'Ayurvedic breakfast serum'*.

Evening:- (at least 2-3 Hrs. before dinner)

- Both Pranayama Asanas (Step#1 & #2)

- Both the Yoga Asanas (Step#4 & #6)

Dinner:-

Consume the **'Ayurvedic Bedtime Serum'** for Dessert or 10 min. after your dinner.

Before Bedtime:- (at least 1 Hr. after dinner)

- Bhastrika Pranayama (Step #1)

- All the Mudras (at least 5 min. each) (Step#3, #5 & #7)

Advait

- Shavasana (Step #8)

In Bed:-

-Practice the 'Pre-Sleep Breathing Routine'.

Want to read more?

Get the book here:

https://www.amazon.com/dp/B07F5YDYH6

27131477R00073

Made in the USA
Middletown, DE
18 December 2018